God Keeps His Promises

First Inspirational Press edition published in 1998.

Inspirational Press
A division of BBS Publishing Corporation
386 Park Avenue South
New York, NY 10016

Inspirational Press is a registered trademark of BBS Publishing Corporation.

Published by arrangement with Concordia Publishing House, 3558 S. Jefferson Avenue, St. Louis, Missouri 63118-3968.

Library of Congress Catalog Card Number: 98-72390

ISBN: 0-88486-213-5

Printed in Mexico.

God Keeps His Promises

Beginning Bible Stories by
MARY MANZ SIMON
ILLUSTRATED BY DENNIS JONES

Send a Baby
(The Birth of John the Baptist)

A Silent Night
(Christmas)

Follow That Star
(The Wise Men)

A HEAR ME READ GIFT COLLECTION

*An Inspirational Press Book
for Children*

To the Adult:

Early readers need two kinds of reading. They need to be read to, and they need to do their own reading. The Hear Me Read Bible Stories series helps you to encourage your child with both kinds.

For example, your child might read this book as you sit together. Listen attentively. Assist gently, if needed. Encourage, be patient, and be very positive about your child's efforts.

Then perhaps you'd like to share the selected Bible story in an easy-to-understand translation or paraphrase.

Using both types of reading gives your child a chance to develop new skills and pride in reading. You share and support your child's excitement.

As a mother and a teacher, I anticipate the joy your child will feel in saying, "Hear me read Bible stories!"

Mary Manz Simon

Send a Baby

Luke 1:5–25; 57–64

(The Birth of John the Baptist)

For Hank
Psalm 104:33

"I want a baby,"

said Elizabeth.

"I want a baby,"

said Zechariah.

Elizabeth and Zechariah
prayed to God.
Elizabeth and Zechariah
prayed to God for a baby.

"I want a baby,"
said Elizabeth.

"I want a baby,"
said Zechariah.

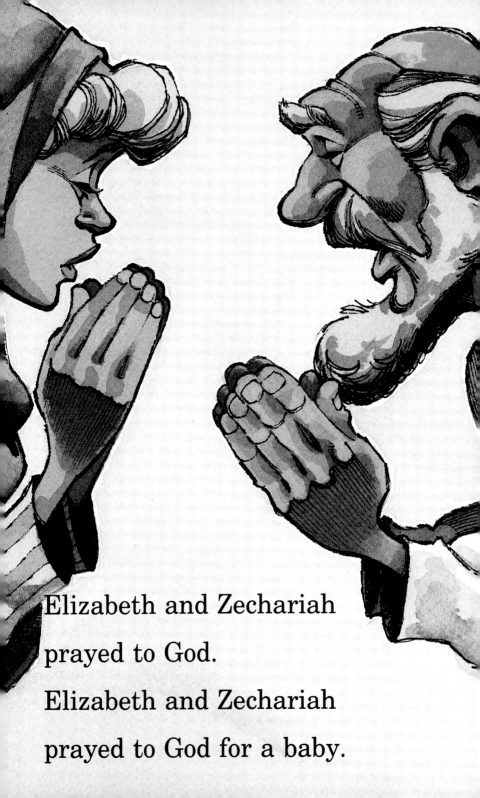

Elizabeth and Zechariah
prayed to God.
Elizabeth and Zechariah
prayed to God for a baby.

Will God send a baby?

Elizabeth and Zechariah
prayed and prayed.
Will God send a baby?

"God will send a baby.

God will send baby John.

A Silent Night

Luke 2:8–20
(Christmas)

"Go," said the angel.

"Go look at Jesus."

"Baa, baa," said the sheep.

"Coo, coo," said the birds.

"Hee-haw," said the donkey.

A silent night.

A holy night.

"Jesus?" said the shepherd.

Follow That Star

Matthew 2:1–11

(The Visit of the Wise Men)

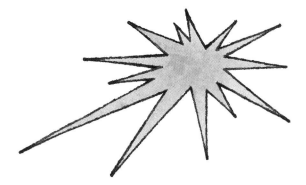

See that star sparkle?

That star is for Jesus.

Let's follow that star.

They rode to see Jesus.

That star!

That star!

Merry Christmas!

There is no secret to our wish -
to give you joy, health and bliss
May your fun be on the sunnyside
this happy, merry Christmastide.

CROWN CITY DAIRY
Valleymaid Creameries

A Merry Christmas

December 25

BOYS' LIFE

THE BOY SCOUTS' MAGAZINE

Christmas
Number
10 Cents

The Community
Christmas Tree

- A Sign of
The Times

Will there be a Victrola in your home this Christmas?

You can search the whole world over and not find another gift that will bring so much pleasure to every member of the family.

CHRISTMAS GREETINGS

Xmas is here
The pleasure's
mine
To wish you
Joy
This Xmas
time

Vol. X   DECEMBER 1902   No. 2

SUNSET

A MAGAZINE OF THE BORDER

CHRISTMAS NUMBER

Bru.

SAN FRANCISCO CALIFORNIA
Chicago·193 Clark St.   London·49 Leadenhall St.   New York·349 Broadway

Christmas Number

Judge

DECEMBER 6, 1919

PRICE 10 CENTS

Drawn by Guy Hoff

"FOR HE'S A JOLLY GOOD FELLOW!"

December, 1911
Fifteen Cents

The Curtis
Publishing Company
Philadelphia

This is just to say
We don't forget
you on this Christmas-day.
May it be a Happy one!

Christmas Greetings

THE SEASONS GREETINGS

COPYRIGHT 1909 ROTH & LANGLEY N.Y.

PLAYING SANTA CLAUS

ALL CHRISTMAS JOYS BE THINE

For you this gladsome Christmas
May joy's fair star shine clear,
And happiness and peace abide
Through every coming year.

34

The Gift for all the Family

With this incomparable instrument of music in your home "all the music of all the world" is yours to command. No other gift can assure so much in genuine delightful pleasure and entertainment, for so long a time, at so little cost, as a Columbia Grafonola.

Columbia

GRAPHOPHONE CO., Box L-270, Woolworth Building, New York

Toronto : 365-367 Sorauren Ave.   Prices in Canada plus duty.   Dealers wanted where we are not actively represented.   Write for particulars.

Any one of 8500 Columbia dealers will gladly demonstrate any Grafonola, from the one at $17.50—and it's a real Columbia—to the magnificent model at $500. A small initial payment places any Columbia in your home—and on Christmas morning if you wish. Balance can be paid, at your convenience, after the holidays.

We illustrate the new "Leader" Columbia Grafonola, typical of every other Columbia in its wonderful tone-quality. The "Leader" equipped with the new Individual Record Ejector, an exclusive Columbia feature.
Price, $85; with regular record rack, $75. Others $17.50 to $500.

COLGATE'S
CHRISTMAS SUGGESTIONS

Cut Out This Christmas List to help you with your shopping:

For Him:
Rapid Shave Powder
Shaving Stick
Perfected Shaving Cream
Talc Powder (the "finish" of a perfect shave), either scented or unscented
Lilac Imperial Toilet Water
Ribbon Dental Cream
Pine Tar Soap—for shampoo
Big Bath Soap

For Her:
A Colgate Gift-Box (3 styles: La France Rose, Éclat, Monad Violet)
Florient—Flowers of the Orient—a new Colgate perfume, daintily packaged
Colgate Toilet Waters—of many different perfumes — you may select her favorite
Colgate's Cold Cream—in Jars for the dresser, Tubes for travel
Charmis Face Powder—an exquisitely fine Poudre de Riz
Talc Powder—6 perfumes and Unscented
Sachet Powder
Ribbon Dental Cream
Eclat Soap
Cashmere Bouquet Soap
Natural Violet Soap

And for the Children:
Young Peoples' Perfumes
Miniature Perfumes
Remember to get for their stockings big tubes of Ribbon Dental Cream
Write to Colgate & Co. for a free copy of the merry "Jungle Pow Wow" book for the top of the stocking

COLGATE & CO.
Dept. L, 199 Fulton St., N.Y.

COME IN Full line of Holiday Gifts

A COLGATE CHRISTMAS IS A MERRY ONE

A Delightful Toilet Water
He will like this
An Exquisite Perfume
Colgate's Gift Box
Cleanliness Comfort Charm
For the Children
A Dainty Gift

Woman's Home Companion

December 1924   Fifteen Cents

Christmas Number

The Crowell Publishing Company

Waterman's Ideal Fountain Pen

In the Stocking of the World

Cut-outs for the Tree

Gay baskets for popcorn and candies

PAINTED BY
JOHN RAE

For the doll's tree

The strips forming the
border are the basket handles

For details about making
these baskets see opposite page

With Best Christmas Wishes

A Merry Christmas to you.

A JOYOUS CHRISTMAS

A Christmas Wish
for my Son!

WM. H. ZINN.
Connecting Stores,
Washington St., Temple Pl., & West St.,
OVER. BOSTON.

Forbes Co.

51

JUNIOR HOME

25c

for Parent and Child

DECEMBE
1932

ONA GALE

ARGARET E. SANGSTER

hristmas Stories

d

andwork

BEN
TON

Interwoven

Toe and Heel

Socks

REGISTERED UNITED STATES PATENT OFFICE

WHEN THRU THE KEYHOLE I DO PEEP
I WANT TO FIND YOU TIGHT ASLEEP.
.MERRY CHRISTMAS.

ARCHARENA COMBINATION GAME BOARD

SANTA CLAUS: I WAS SO GOOD A TRAVELER LAST CHRISTMAS THAT MY FRIENDS CALLING FOR ARCHARENA BOARDS (And Their Name is Legion) INSIST ON MY TRAVELING ALL THE BALANCE OF THE YEAR, AND THE ARCHARENA CO. ARE GETTING OUT A BOARD EVERY TWO MINUTES.

FIVE CLASSES—THIRTY-TWO GAMES.
(SEE NEW LIST.)

1—Crokinole and Kindred Games — 1. Crokinole. 2. Archarena. 3. Ditch Carrom.

2—Four-Pocket and other Carrom Games .... — 4. Four-Pocket Carrom Game. 5. Walk-Around Carrom Game. 6. Billiardette (new). 7. Shooting the Wild Ducks (new). 8. Game of Forty-Six, pockets numbered, (new).

3—Ten-Pin Class of Games ...... —9. Ten-Pins. 10. Nine-Pins. 11. Cocked Hat. 12. Cocked Hat and Feather. 13. Five-Pin Cuban Carrom (new). 14. Childress (new). 15. Five Back. 16. Head Pin and Four Back. 17. Seven Up, Seven Pins.

4—Checker Board Games .... —18. Pyramid Checkers (new). 19. Diagonal Checkers (new). 20. Regular Checkers. 21. Chess. 22. French Checker-Board. 23. Backgammon. 24. Russian Backgammon.

5—Other Original Games .... —25. Flags of the Nations (new). 26. Hawk and Sparrows (new). 27. Shovel-Board Game (new). 28. Spinoza with Tops (new). 29. Ten-Pin Top Game (new). 30. Spinette (new). 31. Single Entry Posting (new). 32. Double Entry Posting (new).

See other side for our Beautiful New Game of Flag Travelettes or Flags of the Nations. A 10c. Copyrighted Book of Rules for 32 Games, SENT FREE for 2c. stamp to pay postage.

MANUFACTURED BY ARCHARENA CO., PEORIA, ILLINOIS.

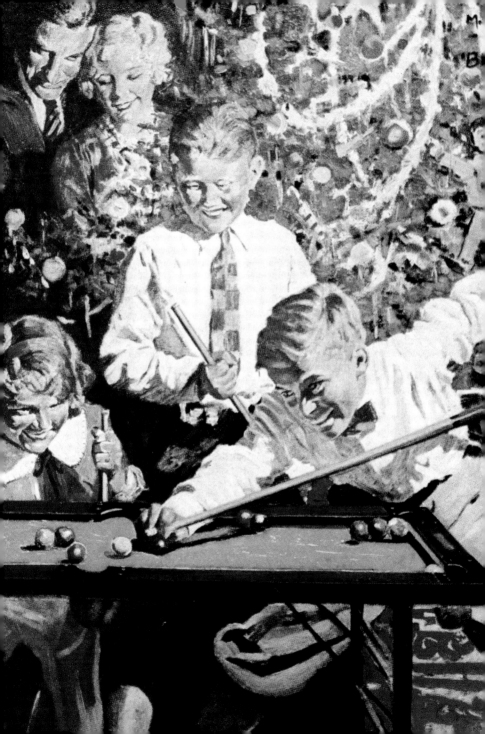

A Christmas Tree for the Dolls
By Eleanor Colby

HERE is a Christmas tree all ready to be hung with toys, and here are the toys all ready to be hung on the tree—and that is a pretty good combination.

First cut out the tree and paste it very neatly to a piece of paper nearly as large as this page. Then lay the sheet you have pasted under some heavy books while you cut out the toys and the decorations. Take plenty of time to do this and use sharp scissors.

When you have everything very neatly cut you may arrange the presents on the tree in just the way you like best, placing the large things, such as the hobby horse and the sled, under the tree.

If you wish to make your tree particularly grand you may cut tiny little bits of tinfoil, tinsel or gilt paper and paste them on.

The grown-ups will wish they were children when they see what fun you are having.

(Page 27)

Holiday Seals & Decorations

THE ART SHOP
8 Barclay Street

COLGATE'S
for Christmas

Useful Gifts
—Not Gimcracks

Cashmere
Bouquet
Toilet Soap

COLGATE & CO.
Perfumers
New York

CHARMIS
COLD CREAM

CASHMERE
BOUQUET

COLGATE & CO.
Perfumers
New York

FLORIENT

SPLENDOR
FACE POWDER

COLGATE'S
RIBBON DENTAL CREAM

COLGATE'S
SHAVING
STICK

RIBBON
DENTAL
CREAM

COLGATE'S
SHAVING
STICK

THE true spirit of all Christmas
giving is to make gifts which
show thoughtfulness and purpose.

For man, woman and child you can
find Colgate Comforts which make
charming, acceptable and useful gifts
— conveying more lasting pleasure
than useless "gimcracks."

However little you pay you are pur-
chasing quality. "Colgate" on toilet
articles corresponds to "Sterling" on
silver.

Join the Society for Promotion of Useful
Giving — be a "SPUG" and select from the
Colgate assortment at your dealer's.

COLGATE & CO.
Established 1806   New York

American Boy

Founded 1827

As for the Wise Men,
    lifting up their eyes,
  A guiding star shone in the Christmas skies
   On your uplifted heart this Christmas Day
May Peace and Joy shine down to bless your way

Merry Christmas
to a Dear
GRANDCHILD

Shop Early at
THE ART SHOP
8 Barclay Street

DECEMBER 19, 1937

The December 15 Cents
American
Magazine

HARRIGAN·OF THE ROCKIES
A Short Romance by the author of "Bamby"

Wish you a Merry Christmas
And Happy New Year too,
Hope you'll like this gift, because,
I picked it out just FOR YOU.

A MERRIE CHRISTMAS

Life

15 CENTS

★

Decemb
1931~

WHAT I THINK OF SIDNEY LENZ · by Ely Culbertson

A HAPPY XMAS

To Wish You a Merry Christmas

Christmas Greeting

*Wishing you Health, Happiness,
and all the compliments of this
Joyful Season*

The Season's Greetings
of Joy and Good Cheer

JUNIOR HOME

The Magazine For Parents and Children

DECEMBER, 1930—25c

WITH BEST WISHES FOR A MERRY XMAS

FROM

CHRISTMAS GREETIN

GREETING

ERRY CHRISTMAS

reetings

MY BEST
WISHES
FOR A
MERRY
CHRISTMAS

Munitions of Happiness

Whitman's

for Christmas at home or in camp

Old General Santa Claus is this year called upon to wage a more strenuous campaign of kindness than ever before. Whitman's candies are his most effective "ammunition" for carrying brightness and pleasure throughout the world, each package conveying, in its sweetness, an unmistakable message of good cheer.

There will be a shortage of really good chocolates and confections, so we suggest that you see *now* the dealer near you who is your Whitman agent, usually the leading druggist, and arrange for your own gifts at home or abroad. We suggest those favorite standard packages

THE SAMPLER, assorted chocolates and confections, one, two, three and five dollars a box.

NUTS, CHOCOLATE COVERED, 50 cents, $1.00, $2.00, $3.00 a box.

PINK OF PERFECTION, chocolates or confections, $1.25, $2.50 and $6.00 a box.

SUPER EXTRA CHOCOLATES or CONFECTIONS, in half pound to five pound boxes, at 90 cents a pound.

LIBRARY package, a de luxe chocolate assortment with a book. Two pound size $2.00.

SERVICE CHOCOLATES, our new soldiers' and sailors' assortment is a favorite gift to, or from, a man in the Service. Each box contains a pound of very special chocolates and a book. Such authors as Kipling, DeMaupassant, Conan Doyle, Hugo. One dollar a box. Our agents will attend to the mailing for you, or we will do so, on receipt of $1.00 and parcel postage.

Write for booklets of standard and fancy packages, or get these from our agents, and plan for

The CHEERIEST CHRISTMAS POSSIBLE

STEPHEN F. WHITMAN & SON, Inc.
Philadelphia, U. S. A.
Makers of Whitman's Instantaneous Chocolate, Cocoa and Marshmallow Whip.

NOTE:—The prices given above may be advanced slightly by dealers on the Pacific Coast and other distant States.

© 1917
S. F. Whitman & Son, Inc.

The Greatest Gift of all is *Health!*

This Christmas, Give a Box of Rich-Juiced
Sunkist Seedless Navel Oranges
(Now Specially Featured by Your Dealer)

WHAT could better express the warmth of holiday greetings than a box of Sunkist California Oranges—time-honored Christmas fruit!

Golden-skinned—rich with the extra wealth of flavor bestowed by all-year sunshine—they carry in appearance, in taste, in thought, the wish for a happy, healthy year to come.

The Cost Is Reasonable

Sunkist Oranges are plentiful now. Dealers' prices suggest the answer to *several* gift list problems.

Just be sure you order the Sunkist kind. The California Navel Oranges now in season have no seeds—are easier to peel, slice and segment—have *more* of the soluble solids for healthfulness and flavor.

Sunkist
Seedless Navel
Oranges
FROM CALIFORNIA
RICHER JUICE . . . FINER FLAVOR
EASIER TO PEEL, SLICE AND SEGMENT

Two Ideal Christmas Gifts

Give a Sunkist Electric Fruit Juice Extractor, the quick way to whisk out juice—and get more of it! Two models—at your dealer's or sent direct. *(Left)* Sunkist Junior: ivory glass bowl, chromium finish body, black base. Only $12.95, delivered, U. S. *(Right)* Sunkist Juniorette: small but sturdy. Complete with strainer and glass, $6.95, delivered, U. S.

All Four Protective Food Essentials

They give you all four of the now-known protective food essentials—vitamins A, B and C, and calcium. Guard teeth and gums. Aid digestion. Build up the alkaline reserve in a natural way.

So buy a box also for yourself. Start drinking two glasses of fresh Sunkist Orange juice every day—*for vigorous health.*

FREE—Recipe and Health Booklets

Many delightful fresh fruit drinks are included among 200 ways to serve oranges and lemons in the booklet, "Sunkist Recipes for Every Day." The place of citrus fruits in the healthful diet is fully discussed in "Fruits That Help Keep the Body Vigorous." Both free. Write address below. Copr., 1933, California Fruit Growers Exchange.

ADDRESS—CALIFORNIA FRUIT GROWERS EXCHANGE
DEPT. 112, BOX 5030, METRO. STATION, LOS ANGELES, CALIF

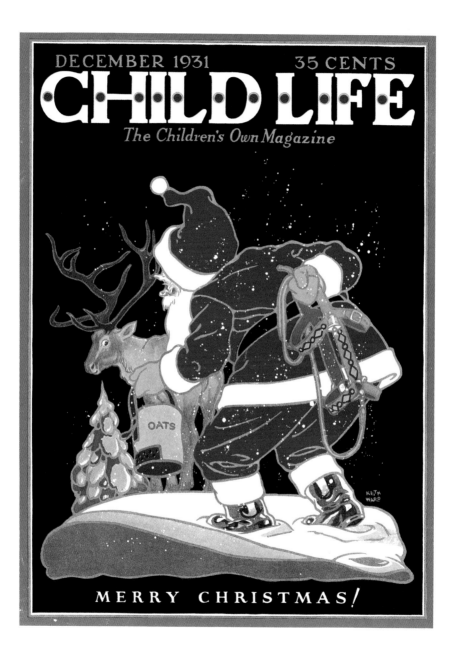

COUNT YOUR BLESSINGS INSTEAD OF SHEEP

Paramount Presents

IRVING BERLIN'S
White Christmas

in

VISTAVISION

Color by
TECHNICOLOR

starring

BING CROSBY · DANNY KAYE
ROSEMARY CLOONEY · VERA-ELLEN

Produced by Robert Emmett Dolan · Directed by Michael Curtiz

PRICE
50¢
in U.S.A.

COUNT YOUR BLESSINGS INSTEAD OF SHEEP · LOVE, YOU DIDN'T DO RIGHT BY
ME · THE BEST THINGS HAPPEN WHILE YOU'RE DANCING · SISTERS · SNOW
CHOREOGRAPHY · THE OLD MAN · WHAT CAN YOU DO WITH A GENERAL
GEE, I WISH I WAS BACK IN THE ARMY · MANDY · WHITE CHRISTMAS

IRVING BERLIN
Music Corporation
1650 Broadway, New York 19, N.Y.

It's Christmas

Christmas
Greetings
I bring

A Jolly Christmas

THERMOS

BRAND VACUUM WARE

Gifts for everyone on your list

THE AMERICAN THERMOS BOTTLE COMPAN

NORWICH, CONNECTICUT • THERMOS BOTTLE CO., LTD., TORONTO • THERMOS LIMITED, LOND

RUDOLPH THE RED-NOSED REINDEER

By JOHNNY MARKS

PUBLISHED FOR

Song
Song (Children's Edition)
Piano Solo (Simplified)
Accordion Solo
Children's Accordion Edition
Organ Solo
Steel, Electric Guitar
Dance Orchestra
Quickstep Band
   (Standard Band)
   (Symphonic Band)
Concert Band
Can be used with Chorals
   (Full Band)
   (Symphonic Band)
Vocal Orch. F & B♭
Two Part Voices (SA)
Women's Voices (SSA)
Men's Voices (TTBB)
Mixed Voices (SAB)
Mixed Voices (SATB)

With Piano Accompaniment
B♭ Trumpet
E♭ Alto Sax
Trombone or Cello
B♭ Clarinet or B♭ Tenor Sax
Violin, Flute or Oboe

ST. NICHOLAS MUSIC INC.
1619 BROADWAY,   NEW YORK 19, N. Y.

FROSTY THE SNOW MAN

Words and Music by STEVE NELSON and JACK ROLLINS

HILL AND RANGE SONGS, INC.
407 COMMERCIAL CENTER STREET
BEVERLY HILLS, CALIFORNIA

The Truth about···
Santa Claus

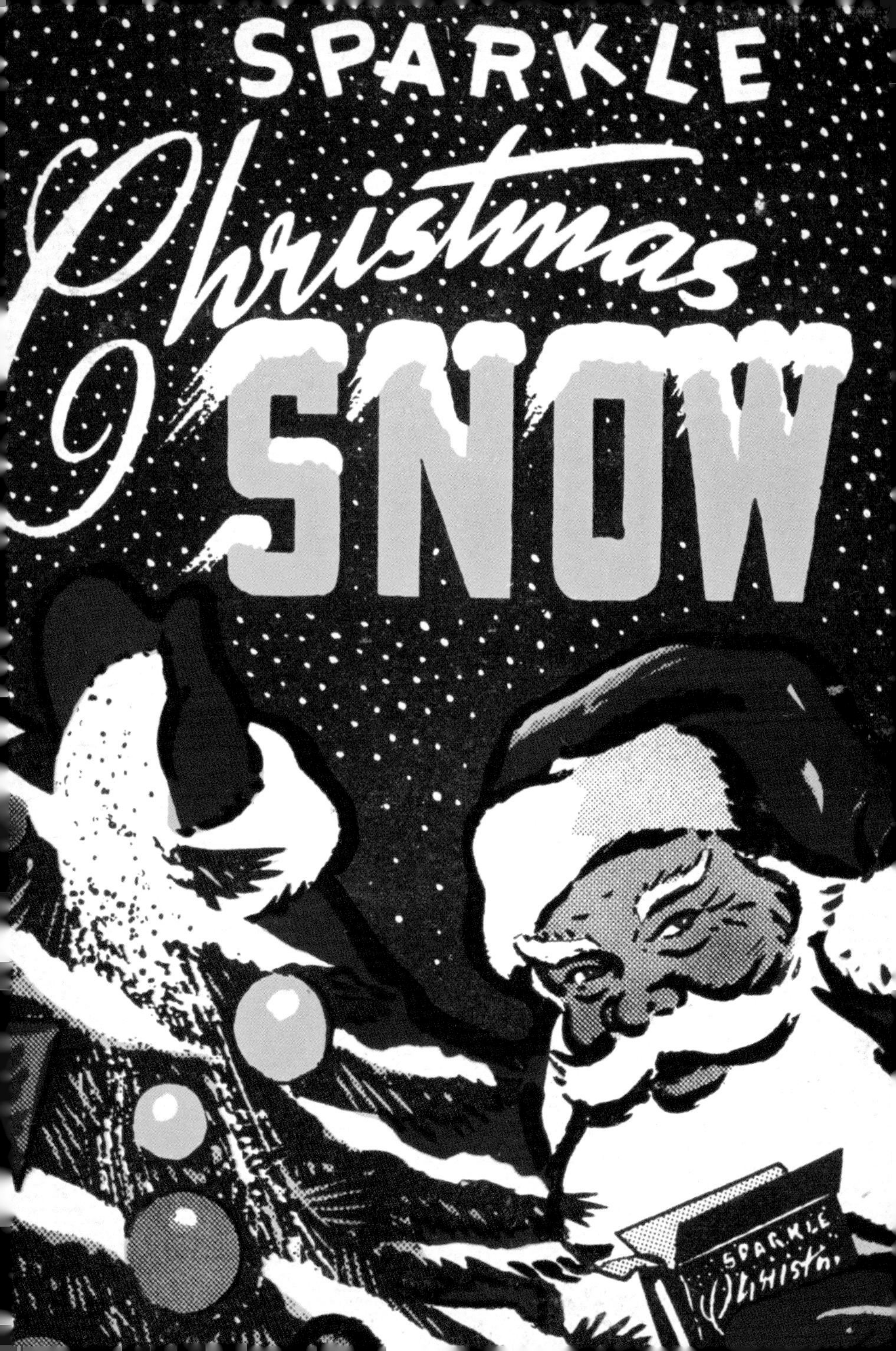
SPARKLE
Christmas
SNOW
SPARKLE

Season's Greetings

the BROADWAY
Southern California

You can be _sure_...if it's

Westinghouse

Even Santa can forget the time when he's listening to this Westinghouse radio-phonograph. And when you play Santa this Christmas, remember, with a Westinghouse radio you can be sure of giving the highest quality performance plus the very best in cabinet design and craftsmanship! The model 190 shown here has exclusive Westinghouse features . . . Plenti-power . . . genuine Rainbow Tone FM . . . a high quality record player that handles 10- and 12-inch records quickly, smoothly, automatically. Yes, the 190 is a leader in its price class. Home Radio Division, Westinghouse Electric Corp., Sunbury, Pa.

Listen...and you'll buy **Westinghouse**

Tune in Ted Malone every morning Monday through Friday ABC Network

WOOLWORTH'S Happy Time
Christmas Book 1952

A TRIP IN SANTA'S RIBBON CANDY ROCKET

SANTA'S TOY AND GIFT CATALOG

1957 - 1958

Santa's Workshop   North Pole, New York

Doubl✳Glo
Icicles
in NEW
Convenience Pack

Flameproof ✳ *Tangle free* ✳ *Lightweight*

BONUS INSIDE

6 CHRISTMAS ORNAMENTS
for package or tree

CONTAINS NO LEAD
FOR DECORATIVE USE ONLY

STRANDS
18 IN. (1½ FT.) LONG

128

What size chair do you wear?
The BarcaLounger is built for talls, mediums, shorts. Be sure *you* get a correct fit.

This **270-S-1 BarcaLounger** is finished in gold-threaded Forest Green tweed. Also available in many other attractive decorator fabrics, colorful plastics and genuine leather.

Patented Model 505 Decorator Series. Modern graceful styling. Chair illustrated is covered in nubby textured Coral mohair frieze. Many fabrics and colors to choose from.

MERRY CHRISTMAS

MASON
COUNTY
PRODUCTS

CE BLDG.

WELCOME TO
"CHRISTMASTOWN U.S.A."

SANTA CLAUS LAND

SANTA CLAUS INDIANA

THE GAY *Funland*

FOR THE CHILDREN AND THE YOUNG-IN-HEART

WHERE THE

Christmas Spirit

LIVES ALL THE YEAR!

MILES KIMBALL COMPANY
KIMBALL BUILDING - OSHKOSH, WISCONSIN

SAXOPHONE PARTY HORN
Red, yellow or green . . . with two pouches of candies and two lollipops. 9½" long.
29¢

SOLDIER AT ATTENTION!
He holds rifle and 3 pops. Yellow or white with colorful trimmings. 4" tall.
10¢

SANTA RIDES IN THE SOAP BOX DERBY!
His car's wheels turn! 8 pops. 5¼" long.
39¢

CHRISTMAS TOYS
and
DEE-LICIOUS CANDIES
all in one!

LINE UP TOY SOLDIERS...BEAT DRUMS...TOOT SAXOPHONES! ALL BRIGHT PLASTIC WITH DELICIOUS, CELLO-WRAPPED POPS AND HARD CANDY!

YOU CAN PLAY THIS DRUM!
Comes complete with two drum sticks. Holds six pops and two pouches of candies. 4⅛" diameter.
49¢

SPOTTED GIRAFFE ON TURNING
Carries two packs of hard candies, six pops. 7½" tall.
39¢

PRICES slightly higher in South and West

BIG STOCKING, 8 TOYS, CANDIES!
Pistol, cowboy, snowman, Santa, soldier, cut-out game, etc. 15 pops. 2 packs of candies. 17½" long.
98¢

REINDEER PULLS SANTA IN WAGON!
15 pops; two pouches of candies. 8" long.
59¢

Made by E. ROSEN CO.

LIGHT UP WITH *Safety*

GENERAL ⊕ ELECTRIC

MAZDA CHRISTMAS TREE LAMPS

STAY BRIGHTER LONGER

"LUMINOUS" CANDLES
...Candle-shaped bulbs that glow from tip to base with rich color. For use in both series and multiple strings.

"ELECTRIC" CANDLES
Small candles, with tiny electric lamps, that sparkle like the old-fashioned tallow candle. For series strings only.

For a glowing Christmas tree, use General Electric MAZDA lamps . . . and watch young eyes sparkle as these famous lamps light up. G-E lamps do not burn out quickly . . . nor do they lose their brilliant color. (Standard colors are white, red, blue, green and orange.)

Not only will you light up for beauty, but the safeguards of General Electric manufacture and tests eliminate the hazards sometimes found in inferior bulbs. Why risk spoiling your Christmas when G-E Lamps stay brighter longer—and are safer?

General Electric makes only the bulbs. For best results you should insist that outfits and other lighted decorations be equipped with General Electric MAZDA Christmas Tree lamps. *And be sure, too, that spares and renewals bear the G-E trademark.*

"MULTIPLE" XMAS TREE LAMPS . . . In multiple strings all the lamps do not go out when one lamp goes dead, as they do in series strings.

"STANDARD" PINE CONE SHAPE . . . comes in white, red, blue, green and orange. For series strings only.

144

THE LOITERER

WOULD you hold Christmas longer—make its pleasures last and last—stretch its joyous spirit over all the months for years to come? Then make an investment in radio. It will bring you returns in unnumbered hours of wonderful entertainment out of all proportion to the money you will spend.

Like the Magic Carpet of Bagdad, it will whisk you through space to distant cities where the famous in music hold thousands breathless—vocalists who command a king's ransom for a song—instrumentalists whom the world delights to honor—renowned symphony orchestras interpreting the great vi-

sions of the masters—famous bands that set your pulses dancing and your feet tap-tapping.

A turn of a knob and you are in another great city, listening to the nation's leaders of politics, science, literature. Another turn

EVEREADY HOUR EVERY TUESDAY *at* 9 P. M.
Eastern Standard Time
For real radio enjoyment, tune in the "Eveready Group."
Broadcast through stations—

WEAF	New York	WFI	Philadelphia	WCCO |Minneapolis St. Paul
WJAR	Providence	WGR	Buffalo	WOC	Davenport
WEEI	Boston	WCAE	Pittsburgh	KSD	St. Louis
WTAG	Worcester	WSAI	Cincinnati		
		WWJ	Detroit		

and you are in a stadium seat watching gridiron gladiators battle while partisan college cheers split the air—or you are in the bleachers shrieking with the crowd that supplicates Casey for "a hit."

There are many fine radio receivers from which to choose. There are prices to fit every purse. Near you are dealers who will give you expert advice, install your set correctly, and furnish you with reliable accessories.

EVEREADY
Radio Batteries
—they last longer

Manufactured and guaranteed by

NATIONAL CARBON COMPANY, INC.
New York   San Francisco
Canadian National Carbon Co., Limited, Toronto, Ontario

148

Merry Christmas

Christmas Carols

for all to sing!

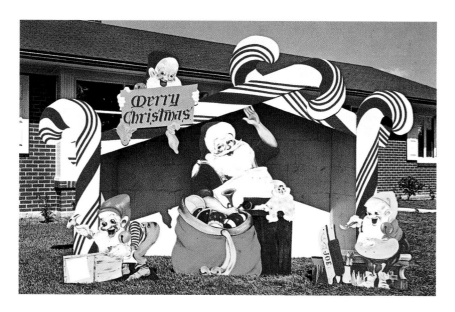

*Merry Christmas
to Grandfather*

SP 208 The best of wishes for Christmas and the New Year

SP 207 Greetings at Christmas and best wishes for the New Year

SP 230 To wish you a Merry Christmas and a very Happy New Year

SP 219 Wishing you a happy holiday and a very happy New Year

SP 221 May Christmas and the New Year be bright with happiness for you

SP 217 Greetings and best wishes for the New Year

SP 212 May you have a truly blessed and joyous Christmas

SP 206 Have a very happy holiday and an especially Happy New Year

SP 216 Best wishes for a Merry Christmas and a Happy New Year

SP 205 Hope you'll have a Merry Christmas and your very best New Year ever!

SP 223 Greetings and best wishes for Christmas and the New Year

SP 206 Wishing you happiness at Christmas and the best of everything in the New Year

SP 225 (from the TWO of us)
SP 226 (from the THREE of us)
SP 227 (from the FOUR of us)
SP 228 (from the FIVE of us)
SP 229 (from the SIX of us)

SP 228 Warm wishes for Christmas and the New Year

SP 222 Friendly greetings and best wishes for Christmas and the New Year

SP 215 Best wishes for a joyous Christmas and many blessings in the New Year

SP 202 Hi! Have a very Merry Christmas? P.S. And a wonderful New Year, too

SP 218 Have a Merry, Merry Christmas and a very Happy New Year

SP 209 May the wonder of Christmas ever fill your heart

SP 213 Merry Christmas and a Happy New Year

KEEP THIS PAGE

Here's how to make Christmas card selecting much more fun. Save the magazine, mark this page and get the family together. When you've chosen your very favorite Norcross Christmas cards, take this magazine to your dealer to make ordering easier.

Each of the bright and original cards shown here comes in a "Solid Pack" of 25 of the same sparkling design . . . and all are yours for a budget-wise $2.00.

So get several "Solid Packs" of 25 to meet the whole family's needs. Other Norcross "Solid Packs", each containing 25 of one design, range from $1 to $4.75.

Like your name printed inside? It costs only a little extra. Your friends will remember Norcross' brilliant Christmas designs. And they'll remember who sent them.

There's always something New from Norcross

NORCROSS
Greeting Cards
© NORCROSS, INC.

Wee Wisdom

MAGAZINE FOR BOYS AND GIRLS ▶◀ DECEMBER 196[1]

20¢

Santa Claus, Ind.

Ho! Ho! My Little Friend:

It's the week before Christmas, I've been working all year;
My brownies-too, have been busy; just wait till you hear.
We made dolls for the girls and trains for the boys;
Yes hundreds and hundreds of all kinds of toys.
I'm packing my sleigh for that magic flight
From rooftop to rooftop, flying all thru the night.
Down the chimney-I'll come with a bound,
And into your living room with scarcely a sound.
I hope you'll be sleeping snug in your bed,
While visions of sugar plums dance in your head.
Then I'll leave your presents and away I'll fly,
Happy Christmas to you and a Merry Goodbye.

Your jolly old friend.
Santa Claus

Santa's Workshop

What dreams are made of...

A bright, shiny Roadmaster Christmas! The slick-riding bike that has *everything* a boy and girl want... electric horn, brake-operated stoplight, bumpers and Searchbeam headlight. A dream come true!

Just what mom and dad want, too... the extra strength and safety of Roadmaster's 100% electronically welded frame. Write for our free catalog, then see your dealer.

Roadmaster

CLEVELAND WELDING CO., W. 117th St. and Berea Rd., Cleveland, Ohio. Subsidiary of AMERICAN MACHINE & FOUNDRY COMPANY, New York

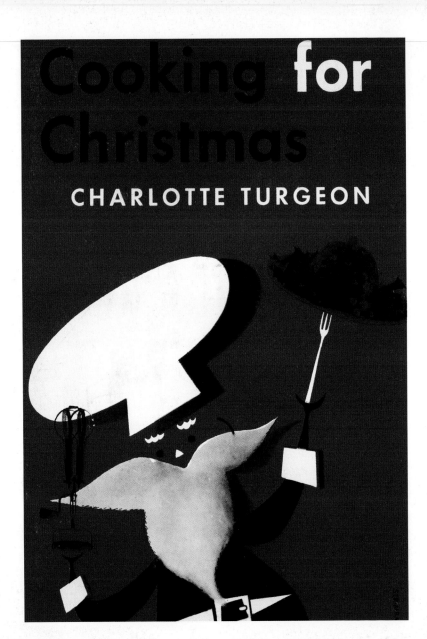

Cooking for Christmas

CHARLOTTE TURGEON

Menus

BEAUTY AND CONVENIENCE YOU'LL ENJOY FOR MANY YEARS

Christmas Trees
and
Christmas Gifts
made with
Reynolds
Aluminum

NEW COLOR MAGIC!

and only Reynolds Aluminum Foil Gift Wrap has it!

Because only Reynolds Aluminum Foil can give you colors that really *glow*. Glittering reflections and light effects to take your breath away! Luxurious textures and designs beyond compare!

NELSON SHAWN PHOTO

From only 39¢ at Variety Stores everywhere including: **F. W. WOOLWORTH, S. S. KRESGE COMPANY, G.C. MURPHY CO., J.J. NEWBERRY,** **BEN FRANKLIN STORES, S. H. KRESS CO., KUHN'S 5-10-25¢ STORES, M. H. FISHMAN CO., MORGAN & LINDSEY, INC., ROSE'S STORES, SCOTT STORES, T. G. & Y.**

Look for these packages when you shop. Generous quantities, wonderful values!

REYNOLDS ALUMINUM FOIL GIFT WRAPS

for those who want to give...in the world's most beautiful way!

REYNOLDS METALS COMPANY, RICHMOND 18, VA., THE WORLD'S LARGEST PRODUCERS OF ALUMINUM FOIL, MAKERS OF REYNOLDS WRAP. SEE REYNOLDS ALUMINUM SHOWS, ABC TV . . . "HARRIGAN AND SON" FRIDAY NIGHTS, "ALL-STAR GOLF" SATURDAYS

trees

become

much

more

Picture *your* Christmas tree—deeply flocked in snowy white or decorator colors. Do it yourself! It's easy, quick, inexpensive with General Mills Sno-Flok. And it's fun!

Sno-Flok works with any exhaust type vacuum cleaner. Just hook up and spray Sno-Flok on your Christmas tree.

Color tablets are included so you can have a Christmas tree in decorator colors. Also, Sno-Flok is fire retardant and prevents needle shedding. It helps your tree stay lovely *so* much longer!

You'll find many other ways to decorate with Sno-Flok, too. Wreaths, table-trees, centerpieces take on new beauty with fluffy Sno-Flok.

Ask for General Mills Sno-Flok at your favorite store.

Sno-Flok kit contains everything you need for a truly stunning Christmas tree.

with **SNO∗FLOK**
A Product of General Mills, Inc.

® Registered trademark. U. S. patent applied for.

Let your fingers do the walking! Any gift worth giving is easy to find when you...shop the Yellow Pages way!

HERTZ

The Christmas They'll Never Forget!

Cadillac

L.

G.

J.

Santa's
surprise
book

to color

Stephens Publishing Co.
Sandusky, Ohio
Printed in U. S. A.

Compliments of

WALGREEN

YOUR CHRISTMAS GIFT CENTER

Acknowledgments

Producing the Icon series with such ease and speed would not have been possible without the help of a group of friends and colleagues whose interest, generosity, and enthusiasm make these projects a true joy. Special thanks to Cindy Vance for lending me items from her collection.

On the TASCHEN side, author, scholar, and creative gadabout Steven Heller continues to produce our words with grace and gravity faster than Mr. Claus can unload a bag of booty, while managing editor Nina Wiener, true to her organizational skills, keeps tabs on who's been naughty and who's been nice. A mug of well-spiked eggnog to Cindy Vance for another joyful design and production job, and finally candy canes all around to Kate Soto and Alison Clarke for their professional help in gathering all the loose ends.

To stay informed about upcoming TASCHEN titles,
please request our magazine at www.taschen.com or write to
TASCHEN, Hohenzollernring 53, D–50672 Cologne, Germany,
Fax: +49-221-254919.
We will be happy to send you a free copy of our
magazine which is filled with information about all of
our books.

Front cover: Postcard, ca. 1924
Back cover: Matchbook, ca. 1928
Endpapers: Wrapping paper, ca. 1954

Editor: Jim Heimann, Los Angeles
Art direction & design: Jim Heimann and Cindy Vance, Los Angeles
Production: Morgan Slade, Los Angeles
Project management: Florian Kobler and Kathrin Murr, Cologne
English-language editor: Nina Wiener, Los Angeles
German translation: Anke Caroline Burger, Berlin
French translation: Lien, Amsterdam

Printed in Italy
ISBN 3-8228-4586-8